ten flapping elbows, mama

ten flapping elbows, mama

khulile nxumalo

DEEP SOUTH 2004

... the twisted nature
of the rose's journey into the earth...

K. Zwide – *Wooden Spoon*

isbn: 0-9584542-6-4

deep south
p.o. box 6082
grahamstown
6140
www.deepsouth.co.za
contact@deepsouth.co.za

We gratefully acknowledge financial assistance
in the publication of this book from
BUCHU BOOKS
and
THE ROYAL NETHERLANDS EMBASSY

 Ambassade van het Koninkrijk der Nederlanden

The author would like to thank the National Arts Council
for a grant to develop the manuscript

Some of the poems in this collection were published in earlier versions in
New Coin, New Contrast, Imago, Bleksem, WK Phoenix, Chimurenga, donga, Tribute, It
All Begins, Glass Jars Among Trees, Mau Mau Poetry Exhibition, Sulfur (USA), Tripwire
(USA), West Coast Line (Canada)

deep south titles are distributed by
University of Natal Press
www.unpress.co.za
books@nu.ac.za

Cover and text design : Paul Wessels

nogwena, jennifer and the childrens

roll call

my sista, gogo nomasakabula, kelwyn,
ari, karen, paso (malume who said look at *doremifasolatido*),
seitlhamo, lisa, robert,
nheti, da one and only general sbu, mahabane,
ntuli (mr no recitations), nokugcina, lamakhosi,
matabane, turner, dangalira,
zini, phalafala, jabulisile,
reagon, rustum, robin,
pernille, kwena and lulama
lapho kuhlangana khon' amadodana le di fila,
the list is longer than distances that got us to scarce places,
we met what we saw a few minutes ago,
and met the eyes that god gave of stevie wonder, when we get
there
i never need to know
how to thank all of you. glory *amen/ingi,* so here
i am...

contents

don't look for my shine anywhere else

(when I grow up I wanna be a performance poet
that really makes the heroes come along)

sing   don't look
for my shine
anywhere here
my troops
have sung out final
their bundles of prayers they were clumsy bugles spirals

                                                                                    outside

a while ago

(what with) so much of the world
believing it is pointless
to be born so that we find out more
i told all the troops from the centre of my centre in the

                                                                veins of my blood

to go their own way now

that droves flap like a pack of cards
that we lived and have worked
in buildings
of boxes

and in the quiet time resound a very familiar layer
of a caking city and crocodiles shine all the fucken' time!

(with saliva drooling from their teeth, the most as you ever

                                                        gone and seen)

everyday

dose of a diet of millennial sense of
light, me i waited here singing i was born for you

against agents of my own nightmares a sizzle that
                        speaks acid in the mouth do you
hear a strain lacking pace spinning disco balls
aimless whirls from windows of computers
tkzee our chemical treaty
with the heaves of our history,

if this is
my last drunken worship of this place
that behaves this

all we were asking for
was another seven million more
people
whose hearts are tighter
like a simile of violence and hope
marechera who said about these sunsets and sunrises
these eyes yearn to eat them
behind orlando power station's two large arseholes
that used to produce an electricity of fumes
and one day was made to fall

all we were asking for
was another seven million feet of soldiers
in the army of children that sprouts
against diminishing shadows of doubt, diminishing

as is true of all
receding things

call it

sweet when we create of each other's
scrapes against the walls of our
foreheads call it sweet when whole wide worlds
suddenly alight and call it hope or *more brazen fires*
to humble the immature shine

to move with the slicing grace of a pissed off venda mother
spacecraft shipping me to
mapungubwe, will tell you life is a journey to some of us
we just came here for the tourney as it rains light years
of an instruction
from a place in outer space, i have seen them

in helsinki
in calgary and even while my tongues swell begotten
as a boil i have seen them
even in london

so many
worshippers of shine i have seen them
like i have seen shining atoms.

Yeoville kites
(apologies to Black Box)

Again homeplace,
Take the world but swallow it, for every other time
You are doing things that are out,

      here come one with a hole of a bullet,
screaming and pulling nets, along with the suburb's
      trees, *can't you see, victory, in the land of fantasy,*
      very very happy, took the reef, and did not get
accelerated or get
ungathered.

We left when Shack was blinking dismissive
as his tips of laughter scatter. Mirrors brought mine
                  all apart,
I pull it all together
again, over a country in the shadow of oranges,
it stands *so like*
tongues of lava.

We sow and pass through, Raleigh's strip of neon
                  sounds
moved into a fretless night extended, continental
            languages augmented
the tones of our own, all the parrots were awake, such
              a small fish

we are
citadel,
a lawn, approximately,
from heaven

the kingdoms of doing for the majority

of them

in the dance hall so small seasoned
parrots pained to the wall,

street corner, then a festival of curving corners, dividing
     life there and then into a kaleidoscope. Point was we
          were love seminal, we campaigned for koffi annan

the days are wearing strawberry attire now, heads or tails.

Phone rings like a ceremony, we call off the crocodiles.

We are leaving yeoville, *again homeplace,*
At the very start of dawn, the shadow of red sun ascension

Massive
Underneath our view.

Newphenomenal, giant flowers

put up
revolutions
in your little life, an ambling question faces you
how are we living,

in the wedges
in the crevices
of broken cities, home of liquid
spiders, on the palms
of the moon!

as diseased mouths breathe war, speak in
the language of unrest or speak like water, dream child
                                        that rough
roads will bring you
to the door
of a little tenderness
little lavish fields, child please dream, your teeth
in the wind, will you
holler

bruised beautiful things

louder
than the tears of films, larger than crowds?

        I heard a secret man
tune spring to the rhythm of his feet –

Today he is a fluorescent
coat in a cage
and a baldhead

he straddles and he floats,
he chooses polka dot
bowties instead.

today he swaps
knowledges for the
childrens; this man so alone in life,

nectar-nipple
or knock knees. he is a jagged revision
the moment's man of a mission –
there is heaviness upon us.

today he stays forgetful
stays very stingy,

bruised friends,
he bruises them in the place.

tonight he's brightening blinded.
tonight he is inviting a bible
that what it has got giant wings.

Thaka ngoaha

Draw my palms out, expose them
Make as many trees, make los angeles cough out its roots
In a blue forest, run amok
With promise and never get tired
Of tailing incantations.

There are no spoors, even the tumult
Of hurricanes
That spin
In your fragrant sway, and me
Perched on its crest
Opening significantly
Dreaming lengthy,

To walk so fully, splayed breadth, on a crescent trail of
                                                    jasmine petals,

To be convened, headway, to be more expanse than all
                                        the memories of oceans,

To have a wrinkled wing that's unhinging,

Tell me how disarmament never fails
to seek me out,

We probably never can tell
when the dangerous ideas
between our ears
will run away

and return as rain stories falling

on the unexpected side, or will
flare up
only to awaken
the dormant hearts of mountains
or plant smiles along protrusions, along crippled hills
or connect the rivers
and ah melt these denim hearts

i love it when you peel off guava sunsets from my lips
when we make our own first drum skin tremors
behind the first
artistic formation, when the snare of your fireworks, my
turning lion,
i love it

when the headlights tell us you're dancing rend
far into the colours of our calling, the eternity of all
round things.

Orlando Stadium

i like the way ex-lover of soccer
rises to meet his neighbour's doves
purple stripe flight, over a train that always goes to town

he has a way has a walk
when chest of earth opens up
wanting to swallow us
in our dreams let's tell come one come all
about the sunken eyes of

our forgotten soccer stars.

he enters and quickly begins
touching at the farthest corners,
he comes here to mow
the humps
in this latest

vacant

stadium,

he has a way with the kick-off spot
to make friends of its refurbished heart, that
look as if – a millipede's coil safe and sound
lessly

finda finda

  finda finda

this one, that one

you are a small permutation when you troped by
small minds, follow the balls and count the paces in
your positions

stretch a sultry leg into
the 1960's, inhale what's the strange powers that
balmed the 1970's,
thereafter trinkets fell
on houses with big windows/ I went under the mines
uphuph' usibonaphi
sijamp' amaprimus stove

nine goals blurred thru the holes in your net
as big as
isigodi sakamaminzela!

Orlando Stadium
you are a hostel,
concentric miasma that flies against gucci sunglasses
over eyes of a glorified ghetto, are you everlasting?
this one?

finda finda finda finda
the tourists have come here

We both page the air and hear
a whole vacant stadium yawn…

ex-lover of soccer was a man i saw
many many years ago
throw spears at tree trunks,
i approached him –

we had Orlando Stadium – he spits it
was trottled here
dug away
and covered with bald concrete

we discovered the limits of our reach
while grandstanding. Even the Pirates and Chiefs
masters game, could not carry the newest size of
                              America and our shadows.

he said he is full and his brains are bloated nowadays

he said when balls bounce
too far way, adorable
they bounce about too much, non-committal

finda finda

finda fumbler.

Benediction

"They hurled insults at the sky..."
Chenjerai Hove – *Shadows*

a wooden spoon in porridge
of yellow mealie meal,
about to bubble boil

in a motivated economy above us like the nature of eagles,

you took it out
with such violence
lump and very disillusioned,

like a winter sun you twist your ways
like a dog that has eaten its feeder. very insignificant

moon is ignored
when sun overpowers
with daylights spreading peacock

you have a life such as busy,
if i were to eat you, i would be eating
an ocean flashing
on the television screen

drenched with shivers
not from the piercing cold

you dangle and wilt with sweat
not from the blistering heat

run an arrogant marathon behind honey coated walls,

balaclavaed thieves

lurking outside your lights, oh you have the buttons to
                                                    provoke

news that
meander inside our ears
and wriggle rivers in the wet tunnels there, we have
                                            bloated stomachs
resilient their ramblings are

so bright unfulfilled and naked,
willing on rounded wishes

in those dark doors we suspect you are forgetting, under the

truncheon of soft socked feet,

forever churning out the wheels of your journeys of silence. We
are left to linger in the suggestions in soft dying voices say
again *Amen.*

            Take a piece clench
outa my mouth, please
leave me my eight fish net strings
I use them to convoke a tenor, and craft beaded
Guitar letters for the hand of a wife

Don't come here howling
these days
cos you realised
the moon is fattening harder now
in tune with the pace of the lump in our bellow,

A wooden spoon
swirling in the porridge
of yellow mealie meal volcano
about to burst bubble and boil

into a helldom so hellish it says end it here and end it
for good,

fully.

Blues Views Burnin'

And i have not
And i have not got
a room with a view of my blues.

        diepkloof sky sheds
        a saxophone hole of air, lands
        right next to your feet
        the disappear

And i have not got a room
with a view of my blues.

        diepkloof sky yawns sunshine
        or lashes scotching tongues
        but dry breeze bra'
        dessicates the leaves too

And i have not got
a room with a view
of my blues.

        it's night now
        diepkloof sky peels off the roof
        just to gossip dark –
        credo mutwa's four-room
        burnin' in '76

        diepkloof sky began to tremble
        says fears for credo mutwa's grim
        brim
        stampede

credo mutwa graveyards
he sees
in a colour tv

And i have not
no, i have not got a room
with a view
for my blues.

Spinas

(da general when he kommands upon an intellijent empire,
com'agen the job of rezerectaz...)

he walks in he walks through me so trance-stic so semiotic so
poetic. casts a fiery light upon the soft handed efforts of my
resi/stances. he has a mercury gel of a smile at the mouth of his
oceanic tongue. his sneezes posses the quite moments, he has
cracked heels. he told me the rumour, circles have no beginning
or end and drew devastation for me. he drew cold razor edges
and stages of corrugated iron production. he was made of pranc-
ing praises and stood there like night unbinding its influences, like
heaven's heat pelting and said – i am a practitioner, where is the
hole, where i step and prod something will follow i am naughty
cosmorpho cycles can walk faster or slower, not at all depending
on us. i am a head that is house of poets, deep as the days to
come, water i want many faces and i am a loser of colours.
flames succeed me.

he discounted the days at the beach front, selling poems, stoned
all child times *immaculata. for parks, arriving so late. for coro-*
brick buses and parched knees. for mzwinki and trampolines, who
bounce and lead me to you, for mgusha for zig-zag for organis-
ing. for the fascinating pendulum, between two one pala we stri-
ated this street.

for cherry fizz pop stocksweet, for jellybabies and the love
between you and baby jub-jub. for sugus suckers. for 10-fours
milky speech for ginger cakes. for slice atchaar for slice mazam-
bane for brown balls called magwinya.

for mshefane, so sorrowful jut stutter. enter the dragon (for

bruce lee), ma-kick and golden fox. for the snake and the eagle's shadow for jacky chan, the apprentice. for benny and betty's journey to town.

forblareflashlightsforhelicoptershoveringforsteelsinsoft
hesteelgrinofasalivatinghippo,forthemetallicaftertaste
ofteargasfortheholeintheheadwherethebatonlanded,for
givingtheperfectbruisethattherubberbullethasleft,foravo
cadogrenadesforthetrenches where the army-trucks also
landed

for possession, for giddy wind, clouds scatter and nightsky sighs
moontime. for bra wally, when he unskins the moons.

for the steelstance we once knew when the arm that poles the
fist, for the unfurling fist for fingers scrapping near an imaginary
sun,

for real raw hollow breeze in the street, for the lung's clear
announcement of their freedom. for rustum's theory of
adjectives ten times ten years on. for berold's praise poem.

attention right-about-turn
for the marching ants.

It's been raining / since seitlhamo and enia

oceans lick us still,
   brick the heart, and
make the insides a static hi-fi, since
near the mountain end some only begin see their feet
and since i am soft and strong
with large eyes that eat
and since empty tins breed brain canker
and since voices drop on like water,
gazing into that bristly centre
of darklights,
since the trouble with the affirmations of the sky
is that they get misinterpreted they get imprecated
since the forest began hoarse singing
and each and every one under their arm carries what is
                                        a feed for his place

and since coming to is a victory
the way through the door has been clarified
we dab with dirty water, and since you walk so slow
or it is too late to tell and since some deny that trains
                                        are the chunk-chunk
sense of it, the story so hard to swallow, they deny
right as five coaches of electric trains fall outa their
perforate weak dreams, and so wake up
frail and tender wanting to touched,
the air was said to be infested, people died in
multitudes, people had nothing left to give. since
coming home is a sky –
that spread forehead like
a sky.

The healers
*(for all of ma' pikinini, as i see kelwyn's **haghia sophia**)*

we are walkers here, sharp heels sharpened on the edges of
grass. people stroke the curve of the earth here, the reason for
rounded circles lives here. know that skies may never reply.
plead and plod raindance, the skies may not reply. sweetness-
es, laying bare the reason of joy , that is approaching here. an
island on a green hand, jonas gwangwa just brassing out. we
arises like a hum, count heads bleeding bright through the ears.

people were healers here. one of them sparks from deep inside.
unfolds slowly to the mellow rays of eyes that are bulged on a
day firm with all the leopard patterns, dreaming was painted
here

healers, drivers of light. gathering all the tributaries, open
hands, to come tend their injuries there. said i came here with a
taste of dry wire scrapping my head. said my head was a late-
comer here. said i left a
storie/stellar. a preparation river.

nothing
happens here,
now i always follow the furrows. i cannot end the seeing
                                                    of furrows.

we awake upward here. look, she beats on the water's skin. a
platform of drama like a new heart, holding a high leaping sun,
commander from all angles, all the way . some realm this is,
always brought forth and quickly taken away. the expanding
piano's soft
tread upon shimmering cymbals. the shining clarinets

that dance baby smiles in miserable air. the
drumtongues, that have thrilling scarifications. pregnant like the
equator. but my mother your grandmother. in the end

we never knew why her lessons ended up colouring my world as
red, white and black and would one day wake me up as a red dog.
it's a reticent picture. unless there is a schedule to the voices that
are calling you

young ones play suckle, itchy milk of green figs from grandfathers
solemn tree. throw sticks on the streams that ran near the pave-
ment. the children laugh, as the sticks ride the waves of rainwa-
ter streams. photons in their breath, sounds of lone intrusive
steps from a far away desert, far away calling them to heal this
world. but nothing happened

     that was all we heard of the library of
                  beat-keepers
as we walked into a voice that starts with a fractured
                           window,
people spoke with rounded corners
of a continent and a meeting of the hungry. so welcome,
                     i bought some tulips

trailers and trailers / bloom and blaze,
you are a trace of countless seeds, incredible beauty, trailers,
trailers and trailers of red crosses

each new day narratin'
the full story
of our *huge* roofed, vaster, cosmos.

The Great Discount

A crescent shaped panga
Bleeds marrow
Drips
Like last trickles of a hard drawn piss,

Against the wire into a fence
It's the lava of hunger
That mumbles up through
The pores of our chapped earth.

For a long time
Our shadows refused to die,
The crescent shaped moon blinking
Dryly at us, who choke in the smoke and point
Fingers after the catastrophe.

For a long time
We spoke with faces leaning away
As dusk poked fingers
Into the sockets of our corrugated shells and smoking
houses,
"let there be light" we croaked a message to the last
semblance
of what remains and what the grabbing was for
that year's greatest discount

daughters, sons,
bones
tried and dried.

We lose an eye but keep the land
there were no lasers, no possessed movement sensors.

We pose like a warrior and a beginner
pondering the escarpment

       hoarse breath loudens (and loudens)
then shoots bullet sounds

We become emblems
driving tankers
thru the grasslands of their cortex,

Crouching

deep in our jagged-dagger dreaming,
we find a thick-cloaked skeleton
of the sunrises that were never to be,
whose impatient roar
we must now explain.

Emva kwelanga
(for Bra Ndoza van Orlando, stepfather)

between my collection of charred tongues and
a winding distance that has
three roads: one lies very broadly, the other's
joined violently to the *mnyamathi* trees, the other's
not even getting near,

i took my eyes out,
dropped
them plop in a green bottle of
Indian Ocean water (turned very red).

so i had no eyes, when I
returned from inside my *helikopter*
without laws

or dogs or protocol, KZN wars/funds for aids straps around
our necks tighter
tighter every passing day and day

the man the flounder
approaches us step by step,
with a photocopied bat through
his chest
he drives black
driving engines –
he's also renewed his eyes

my eyes grew thorns in the water

Ten flapping elbows, mama

"there is the hill now, it stands firm like the will of time
but i will tear it apart and in those days there shall be no
silence"
Mongane Serote – *Behold Mama, Flowers*

throwin' stones
sayin' nothin'

gettin' scared, mother
when it gets shadowless
and cramped

new days new waiting
for the porridge that smells skin tense
come
for me too

tonight
the green still water's in the mood
to throttle
tonight
still waters breathe
in expanding circles, its colours uncertain.

*

the sky is in a cast, the heart
is feverish. yellowbent near myself, bound
my own fulfilment. stalking and falling,
with ripe feet
very afraid of the treble

of their palpitations. trails in the hoarse
forest, distant harmonica skin, such music
in the brains jungles.

*

sleepdry nights
gettin' scared mother
when the floor begins to heave.

hands keep manufacturing gaunt and sour
sentences that walk off the page – i have misplaced

                                                        knees

i have glued hands,

eyelids drop
as
drawl
forms.

*

the pen's under me. it brays rippling and very cold like a goat
                                        under a slaughter's knife
and power,

for all of us

was it ever true
that the pains inside our heads
is insides of our heads
becoming kettles
of boiling questions, violent exits
of a number we can count

on the fingers

*

usthuphazane lo
isidudla sami lesi
ukhombisile lo
umthethi wamacala
umdanyana lo
yena omude kakhulu
uthembisile lo
umngane wendandatho
ucikicane lo, ithemba lami leli, so eternally

now

let me
down
easy

i am already cracked
i am already dislocating
i have two inches of ambition, next to a shopping centre

        let us wave
while there's still jokes
to choke
your anus on

while there is still giddy planes heading for the future
while there is still eyeballs/poems

        up up and away
into a pimpled sky that has holes.

*

there are trains in south africa
backwards and forwards
forwards and backwards
and still look at days with
chameleon eyes, and

trombones and entanglements settled in and
walking oppressed spirits into my eyes, and in front of

my mug

of memories, and headlights and all
the kind of music that brought to the air a new generation

of questions

*

goes
just like

metal dead birds
that can fly
oversea, they are broken
to holes

now we are going to mend
our broken hands we are going to kill the goat,

that some moments are
that some moments are fine
as they are,

metal dead birds, eternal cycles
flying ceaselessly, as always
we sweeping the hallways

we see
with blank eye the love
between ourselves falls
down our painful gurgle,
is flushed down
toilet pipes
to where
we don't
know.

So now
We are going
to mend the tattered
soles and come here very often,

Bring to me
my sponge-headed arrow

that is a mountainous metal door, my sponge headed sprig

Bring to me
new manuals about showing off

that is a neon song sifting between my fingers.

*

The ninth path had been delayed deliberately.
The goat was slit.
The blood was done so many things.
The questions were put aside.
The world was one long *krempelin* itch.

A builder's bible,
mother.

Hoisting this dawn propping it unflinching

To flutter in these skies,

There's a magenta smile, stretched without
revision. A circle of friends – plinth by plinth –
builds resistance, against the viper's hissing speak

a bliss, a bubble drum as you are
coming from very far, flow
return, retrace, bubble
arriving

lemon razors left
United States had left
into the end's ten flap
but then again.

Blistered walls
crumble
across my face

There are **lovepowers** all over the place.

Five hundred thousand centuries

(to khalo, who is preserving his brain)

Which one is going to survive?

When you ever get there
Tell us

Of the uptight spring diligent delegation

Sent to ask god to advance new

Gourds of understanding. They asked for another five
                                    hundred thousand
Centuries to douse the flaming towers of memories,
                                    they even
Offered to batter their fingers, along with gold studded
                                    staffs
That were pecking the sulk on the ground their children
Had hidden
A drawing as a scroll to god

Of bloated stomachs
Skeleton skulls
Glued beneath a pattern of cringed dry leaves
Of indigenous trees, they called the painting winning.

The letter the children sent to god said:

> "Ask us why
> There is loneliness in people
> And we will count
> The sands of the Sahara

Who is going to survive?

dambudzo died
and the ghosts that painted hearses
over Great
Zimbabwe look to me were the same ghosts that
                                    tormented troy,
same ghosts that got stuck in the throat of carthage.

I saw a flick in my dream dambudzo got kicked in a park
                                            in Harare
Behind a bar that has a trail of piss framing its spine

I got the chill spell of sobukwe and hani's gazing ghosts

I got the person with the stature of cyril who is going to
                                            survive

Another 500 centuries another delegation bearing hand
                                        made crafts
And gifts for god, and their children knew it yet

When the wind blows
Don't let it blow your mind
When oldest of the elders howls
A regally grey impish howl

Then you know the road wedges into a point
At the far end
For us all, after another five hundred centuries to go
When we stop digging
in the chambers of our noses
Mining a sense of existence above all

The circumferences that always bring us to this

Tell me
Who is going to survive?

Into the whistle's nostrils

joy has no generation gaps
nor silences in between
like broken denture. No owls'
bleak eyes blinking
when the question in the air
stings in the eye

a grip, the clasp of hands
is so strong
we're stitching the lesion to the rock
no empty *klevaz*
no one had become
hidden schisms, victims or slow songs
simpering like a basket
under a leaking tap –

when the trees begin to speak out
they are saying to the bioscope on the ground
i know you too
even in your dense silence
silence   the bad silence. When it happened

that a mumbling voice swelled inside
the crowd that had brought itself here
here we were about to experience
the pangas of labour. The bleeding
will cease
for some time

naming ceremonies began in a miracle
that had also brought
itself here to welcome dried foliage

reclaim their lushness – *happy bestday*
    happy bestday
    happy bestday to you
    happy bestday sban'sbani (vumani bo?
               vumani bo? do not ignore
my frenzied drumming behind our song – the bleeding
        may not cease until our hearts abandon
their rhythm: *lamazwe*
anomoya ngesaba umoya
    And doors
    of a dream
    are too dark
    when waking life
    demands its own answers too

as to why these newborn babies'
tiny fingers keep poking into
the future's blank screen and trial and error
knocking, (there was a shadow trembling behind
    their pregnant eyes tightly shut
    vibrating with voices like a shrill inside
    the nostrils of this whistle)

    an agony of a twisted trance
inflicted upon identifiers
with human progression. chained and
cemented to rock
come forth
sycophantic vultures
to feed on our vitals

Really these were very strange
children. they bubble truth. no child
ever falls out into a vacuum (the angry spit

droplets of their utterances
fall through the air
and disturb its quiet. when the dream ends another life
must begin – sure we still rotate with earth
to frame the door of this dream
wherefrom torrents of strange children in the strange
situation fell out – one by one

wailing *sokokota thina sokokota thina sokokota*
thina – why because
we must upturn and update this trance tradition

so we are going to upturn and update
with force – poke this rubble and mess
refuse and cobwebs
otherwise without the answers we need
the knocking is an air against words
to be breathed and farted
without odour without meaning

 (this i must tell you, there was
once a time when those who make and give birth to life
were always there, you see it was right here
they mumbled it is sad to see
a lost generation and a generation gap
at the same time. then tu!
silence silence the bad silence.

maybe
their pregnant eyes – our children have
pregnant eyes! but children say
separating tangents from circles
leads to simple frustration
of how it happens – they see how it happens

that electric fire, in thick life size boots
presses your against a corner
scattering liver and mind
swirling
twirling
tornadoes and tides we see we see

and then
there is nothing. why.

you see we – the strange children in the strange
situation
have it scrawled on our forearms
that shut eyes are fire
that what we see is not a creation of a restless vacuum
that we are not making sketches from blind voids

we are going
to poke this rubble and mess
otherwise...
why
because
there are
answers we need.

why won't mongane's stars'
sinister whispers louden tonight
what is fate
if i have one eye
who dons the blame (that cap one size
fits all
those that are
those that have been here
with bigger designer, there is nothing new

about you or us

and waking life is demanding
its own answers and the strange
children begin searching for the
central question

something said during a short break – Motherfly
must be proud
to have thinly escaped the unturnings of the water's
helix
when the spoon snaked into the cup, gasp
so it seems

because everything does
first of all. It seems like
the strange can hear
brains that distil poison
they say they hear fingertips painted red
flailing devilish droplets

(and they wept all the time
inside, each time the blanket of night
falls over the world. they say it pains
to be stagnant with stampede of agony
alive and stomping
against the insides of your heart

or races of squares fitted into crooked
triangles
and confused circles. many many baby
tender minds will hunger strike
when even these grey knuckled wrinkled hands
cup so soon at the face of the little one– *vumani bo?*
Siyavuma!)

so it was pure despair
when many woke up to decide
to hang their nerves, organs and things
on a kilovolt electric pylon

forever and ever

is a spine electrocution that plays back
each time answers staggered tripped
and fell
only to rise up as questions
even the world so big and round
plays *black mapantile*
because it knows you are searching for it
     you walk. it walks too
     you stop. it stops too
     you walk and walk on
    stop. look back
     it is never there
a spine electrocution each time the tv
radio newspaper and gossip never told us
why why why

Another
one of our trial-and-error children is intent
on picking up papers
why sweeping soil of soil to find soil there
when they had resumed to painstakingly study
themselves. the strange children.

why because it came out
much much later that what
is stealing our oxygen is big and has

big arms (open so wide)

like if I am ant, you elephant
what will happen
if I am ant and you elephant erected firm
like an electric pole. swashbuckler child
answered that

      when we are many – the army of
ants
we will crawl up your nostrils past the
hairs and chew the belial in there to
death. we will

      crawl past the cigar smoke
why because ants' persistent determination
is workers who know their story
is workers who listen
to their dream's clang
  strues' god there's millions of us in here
  to uproot

      why because we have once inside a moment
encountered a hoard
of silly beings just like you
donned in fluorescent groping playing
camouflage in the cement bush
just like this belial does
here inside your head there is the answer
to why
answers became
disguised as question – just last year
         when you were hear to experiment
         with sanity we fell hard

from the staircases
        of
           disillusionment

      why because we created you out of that creative
                                  moment
see see
the dongas remaining. not so repairable.

the world rolls
and thieves of dark with it too
having forgotten that all
is guaranteed an appointment with the
kindest sun tomorrow morning...eyes of the world
are rolling now as we speak behind the loudspeaker

behind the loudspeaker are the strange
children,
when they had decided
to shake out the streets
for the whereabouts
of the central question
the central
situation. The Question avalanched
 from nowhere and clubbed us each on the head

only i survived a stray tightrope walker, peripheral
with the mountains, apparently i must tell you this
                              threnody
that is:
      lemini
       iyeza
nakuwe

why i am
in a din and rotting
in the sun still up here
in rubble and bloody fuzzy times
lots of people will live in there again
and again down there, the masters who chose
my matchbox casket are under the sun still
command torrents of acid over the frustration
of numerous things hanging like washing with the discipline
                                                    of nappies

talking to the wind under their wings hanging
on electricity pylons

of this, there, the blurred figures and shapes taking form
the mass of mothers and fathers
is coming
towards me here
to the darklights where light dries and goes and then
days are dark what to do with them darklight brings no
comfort i say even to the one who paints life with a
                                                    sensitive
whisker. yes. we are life the original model of all life
                        form sculptured to figures of
ice. melt. there is no more moss near the tap, for you to
                                                    tell your

lies to

still
mothers and fathers, they
never reverse.
one way. i was given birth to and i am giving birth
still why because all of them hanged on
electric wire so this is why life feels like the longest lesson
on the pliable presence of a stone i was

life steaming baby when we first met, but new eyes and

callow

all of us   forgot
to see your question how
it feels to be born
at the most right time how we lost it too
the end
of drought, one we dreamt
about
once why it throbs to see
a generation gap wilted times
and the ever searching clasps of new generation at the

same time, we are losing

generations each and every time

it is so much
of stories getting retold when

"order is going. there is no place
for a story retold." the mothers and fathers are urgent now

"why because we inhaled it too in past times
the threnody of the future walking through
closed doors and walls. we dreamt
a spectredom vanquished

our children

those that are and those that are gone, come back with us,

it always comes out later that it is pure despair
to never have waited
for the world

outside your head
to come
inside your head
then both move together, yes our world is rolling when
we speak

anything else is pure despair.

Xstacy

Count your nipples scissored
prime time when they're raw raped
by a kentucky fried chicken,
say that's what you
win – a few zero hours zones, white sangomas, pulse
arthritic fingers
pointing
pointing everywhere?

When we waited, intestines nervous
we waited throbbing heat
in our broken heels
from the distance that turns thin pulse of
the little toe into a sting. But
you could fart if you wanted and the mountains
were smiling.

We cast the load back
to the ballot box
of debi demo-
crazy the wind conducted itself
very badly when it set our sight alight with dust in the
excited eyes,

Canned frog toes in telkom bow wrappings were
served to the newcomers we taught them how to
vote they taught us how to wait
in mamba long queues,

It rained glass and *cadbury eclairs* that year.

We on the roof could not stop singing

bleeding still
from the glass grains stuck
between the toes.

The young words of a talkative poem

> *"when your heart swell up till you feel it are go bust*
> *you can't find the rhyme to fit the beat*
> *when you can't find the answer for the puzzle complete"*
> LKJ – *Story*

Everyone dig this There shall be no more tears
For the beacons who fall the easiest

There shall be no more tears, when we all have

these worlds that multiply
as many as the hymns of all our true pronged heads,

Soon

there is for a guy like me
some house to build, some time to choose
living without
loving feeling at the edge of the cliff and blinded youth,
      some time to say simple throw away the little
      of my childhood and all my ideas, and regret
the paintings that etch on the faces of my two
loving-humming
children

who must conquer
crosses in every place
or conquer a country south of Africa, with just my hand
                    to hold. I looked
and all the televisions were letting me down

promise I looked

and went away wobbling to a diuretic dither
when you are as young as me
you see
no stairway that is going to take you there
beyond the point where the cove of questions funnels of a
                              memory trudges past
it's shadow sweaty and weary
because my performances, bitter and bloody, only send
                              a luminous question to you
is it mental or emotional, did the show
give only strident voices with promises in their denotations,
do all our powers fill in for the dry sky of drought, with
                              fabrics of youth as
its torch in the clouds

We came
Here fresh from a round of visitations, to find a length in
                              visions

we came here with pre-meditation
we came here lugging a ball color of a dream, hefty, as we
were suspecting there is no one else upon

                 all the specks of soil in all the world

who is able to be so correct

         If tomorrow is really a child of our sperms today
We are stepping
On frying eggs, sometimes we were very wrong

We come fresh from a tribe called quest to correct or rap
the horizon to which all eyes are locked
only ends when you close the boulders of the bomb bunker

where there shall never be a rustle of love rivers no
       prophetic fit whose mouth spoke bubbles

who are these people

who announce an all we needed to know basis
who said the most prudent thing to keep a secret

was the spoken wheel and who started to relish the trudge of an
evil speech
who were thrilled by a viral intention who turned one and
                  zero the other way around

who were the first to arrive who took the time to know
manipulation

who spent the rest of their life affecting the weather who
                          were
so sure about
notation it is risky to sound so talkative
in this poem our time has become so talkative, what if

in this poem we are talking into a megaphone and we
                       interfere
with the radio?

     all the petrol attendants had no scope
of the details where my reveries were going to sleep, the
                  headquarters

of the project
called the futures that were lost, and learnt
you can lose the protagonist as
you lose these futures, long before it is time

Dig this
Before
We erased it

Talkative like science
claims the rhythm
in the beat of every heart, these are living hearts,

If you plant the right spark
It will travel. I have thrown away
All the fuses, simple, electrical vertical like

Killarney
Old age high rise heaven that can shut its heart
In some days when it's electric eyes get shut
It truly becomes black as the night
The access roads make cars in a city have a churn of blood

Have no fear people at the end of the river
The bones in the inner breasts
Of the oceans are shaking

Have no fear people who have new eyes who have hands
                                    to raise in the crowds
Every speck of talkative colour, each and every sparkle,

Even as there seems nothing in this race but robots and
                                              holograms

Even as hunched up, packed like potatoes in a sack,
listen inside

a minibus hearse, robots, holograms and more corpses

sound like are wailing

a song of silence,

Even as there is a child in your mind who cannot recall

Responding to a call from the seminal scroll. Even as we see no hands to help us get back from the lights that died in our eyes, even as all our beacons ahead find it easiest just to fall, we shall have no fear.

Festina's echo (i'm returning i'm returning i'm returning

First
you said
I breathe brown there a damp earth's
throb you love to knead.

Yesterday clanged and cracked
without you. The wrestler is ridiculous
upon flakes of rocks, reptile style
like a frozen
waterfall,
with big moon beckoning
his backside,

dreams of a fly
feeding rock the tenderness of its abdomen

rock gave back warmth
in return,

I know

What do hearts do
when they eat each other?

Lately
I've been
growing peas and belts
inside a dim lamp, soul fanged
between the very same corrugated walls of madness

oversize shadows skulking over my eyes,

I think I am wrestler thinking of diepkloof's ongoing
dust. The damp clamp of your tentaculate outgrowths
around my
sinking forehead and the way you were

reaching in

eager to spin
Zone 6's foreway sky, my own tired hand/roof
over my poets carpet
does leave the earth.

I met your smell
at the hem of the door, then
you said
you were an unhappy telephone line and mouthed
imprecations about a dismembered core

I brushed past
your chest of choices,
and i got swallowed in – like when you lean
when you take off a decision like you take off your shoes

We loved each, near a straight line
of white tables, a million laughing years which said
it was sore at the ankles and just disappeared
into this the season of hard drivers/ flapping hearts
rough scraping our backsides

le kelesenke. tsena, ke diswitsi tsa lerato, crackling rivulets
crackling favourites, crackling tremendous
disappointation. *ke tlisitse lemmu* from the dead river
I'm returning with echoes and elongations
I'm arriving with the restless trees.

Shafari

(for fathers and sons of fathers in the long line of preachers, Itumeleng)

> *"My father before my father...*
> *with his multiple godhead*
> *sat on his circular stool*
> *after the day was done*
> *at times between the redness of two suns"*

Keorapetse Kgotsisile –
The Present is a Dangerous Place to Live

He sends her dry flowers
He sends 2003 technology love, my friend, sends love

Through the tunnels webbed like nets
Behind his cell's facial design of blink
Blink liquid
Crystal
Display, and gets into my car

we drive making a new map of another invention South
Africa, drive

around a detritus of Africa as a continent of problems
we drive upon
her cities between here and Nigeria

i swear i see bloodroses, as the sun rises,
another pack of surprises,
they have their own

attendant

thorns.

i know we are made from this earth, but
the highways smell of mist of pricks of posthumous
colours.

Oceans, when you have none in Gauteng, seem awash
with the ability to grind us

my good friend and i drive

blind

The red illusions of roses
begin expressing themselves

darkness appears, our shadows
disappear,

we drive
into a skyward monument and aspire
for the Tropic of Capricorn

in limpopo words had voices and eyes

any eye
can lick a mark on tarmac, in the places
of fire the long line of fathers tells us, when you walk
updating the dances of fire
you do get flames growing in your head

as high as the land is tight, as boys
bungi jump
against victoria's fall,

it becomes the glimpse of all we know
of all our stubborn problems

war is not between an eye with a side

not between a foot's savvy when bullets come
unannounced, leaving bitter craters in every side?

war is not with
the other one working out
the mathematics conducting the configuration
of an ever hungry concrete sea

> we drive, one of our country's many
> seas sets us into motion
> among liars
> and trumpets
> of cynics, a teeming
> swarm

> on and on

my friend and me
we drive
licking on.

Gciina

i saw you step
into a star
and
eat it's light

i saw you

i saw
the sea's
storyline
join
your eyes

Festina

I sniffle sunrise, late as usual.

The end of my story's right here
I will roll it into a ball
I will tumble it home like sunsets used to do
Before I told them I come bearing a fiery and effective
Beginning.

I had clutched my donkey
skin blanket, I'm under it
shaking order
into valleys I spread a dancing stripe
like water, then we were drowning and bouncing
on the sea seven metres below a sepia horizon, phlegm,
                    soft hands plaited our dreadlocks
                    into a siamese connection.

there was also a zinc door, my hand
responds
its way
inside
an asthmatic loss
of words…

why does it dive, no matter what

if something burns and bones
fall like leaves
the day you come into me, the day what
you love I flow slowly into

waydown
my throat aghast
lined with furry whispers.

Come in, paraffin lamp
Festina

Take this glass eye
or lay it bare
to burn

remember, midnight
letters are desperate,
cliffhanging,
the thread's about
to snap. Watch me

drag my entrails their
fey moments their shyness to release
the faeces

i sometimes do
i want to

lunge at you
but i stop right before we contact

The world's astir and i'm running
running on their heads running to you my emptiness

tries to become one with me, noises feedback the
walls are laughing everything is here

vagabond shadows

poke us
      do us
            turn us over
                  and get us emptied,

leaking, at times clamped in between
encyclopaedic pages

      they found me crazy and left me
spraypainting corners with images
with images of an unstamped letter to home

      rehearsed
desperate but open
like a steel tablecloth curling up at the edges

      does nothing, when coming home you found
everything shifts
      sun-tense images
for the reluctant ankles.

Sleepstroker

coming in
from near a dream *touch-touching*
bulbs pipes cisterns locks and spikes on the wall
touching
the flute contours of your belly
mumbling secrets
only singing deserts can understand

where the future of this word and the next is
the only distance
between your eucalyptus prayer
and my weeping

it was a familiar place, where salif & angels
& sounding seas meet, where every
note wet with the promise of soft rain sobs
inside bree street public toilets
and a muted horn ignites in blue cyber psychotic space

coming in just in time
for our bodies to conduct jhb as a whole it
glows warm or it yawns at its own skyscrapers, it gives us
only the drudge
of its industrial saliva

the ear becomes faster than the eye
and talking was the slowest movement of them all

i had come

to your breathing belly, refusing to say
which one of us is

chanting with the secrets, face to face with the locus
our bodies and i hear your
insteps very much

pulsate to the rhythm of fufu

around their own
centres of shine.

Craftin'

(a proemdramatic for the Soyuz spaceship and its mission of 2002)

The Cast

NDRAMAS
BENDE
MASSGRAVEDIGGER
A DANCER
A DRUMMER
THE POET
MUSICIANS
THE BIG THICK VOICE THAT WE NEVER SEE

The Introduction

The world ended just yesterday. Only one person survived. She is an old, frail woman, and all that is known of her is that she worked as a mass gravedigger all her life. This story chronicles her rummage through the chaos and the carnage. Two timeless and almost omniscient, very aloof narrators, with the help of dancers, musicians and drummers tell us this foundationless gist of the story of the dead world they never even knew.

The narrators give us off-glimpses of the world that has been lost and ask us to join them as they try to seek out why that world might have had to die. This piece is called a "proemdramatic", after a form originated and developed by the likes of Ingoapele Madingoane with the Mihloti Players and later with the Medupe Players in the 1970's. They called it "proemdra". It is a form that forces prose, poem and drama to talk together as one genre.

The Proemdramatic

(The STAGE IS EMPTY and dim, in the light of an incomplete blue moon. We see the presence of a fresh open grave, dominant in the middle. Ndramas and Bende, dressed in the most colourful of attires, emerge from a dark womb, stroll in, look up and then look through us)

Ndramas (through goggled eyes): Night
        waits for daylight to flatten out and go,
        velvet moths velvet moths
        but look i am flying wide above melting
        trees, above stinking seas,
        i'm hauling stars into my
        rounding heart

(silence)

        and now you with a fruit-basket-full
        imagination...

Bende: But I will be brave
        for you

Ndramas: There's one ocean of pleasure in giving in
        to each other, i am bubbling compulsion,
                              just
        in case my echoing visions cause unrest
        where your nerve motors most digest...

Bende: No I will be brave....

Ndramas: You have that
        bowl only to consume vapour from this,

a wounded dry pool, bleak
like eternity on all ends, ah the distant
stars
we see twitter to and fro tonight ,
writhing full of blinking
hands of songs about us and the many
far away roads with cracks
to travel, roads to which we must look
directly then.....

(They both turn and fix their look to the far way roads ahead of
them. Ndramas strains his vision through the goggled eyes. They
see dance and music wrestle each other, each seeming to be
struggling to follow what the other is saying. The poet tumbles as
she flows upon the stage, coming in)

fragment/peril

1

Histories, pro
verbs pieces
words of parting that end
near a tranquil
silent effervescence, remain
stagn
ant waters

buzzing
with inside life,

words of parting like parting

streams,

words of parting silently like why
dry
rivers
never reach the Oceans. See this.

In the long distance called past
comes a massgraved
igger, frail, bent
and swaying
to the burden
of undep
arted souls that cling
upon her,

gaunt souls addicted to light
pining for a perilous bang, the
loudest exit route out of this undecided place

*(The poet exits, making room for Bende to speak as the dancer
lunges everywhere as if to make us aware that massgravedigger,
who came in as the poet was saying, was last and only person
after the end of the world)*

2

Grey morning,
question mark exclamation
mark dawn
in the beginning/dayness.

We only begin to see her just before that time, our old massgravedigger. She found crumbs, remains, after ashes and embers of a life that was they said it was fiery, now just another dumping site. It was easy to make out most of the memorial platforms, this is the end this was dry earth dry stone dry water

(The dancer is moving like a dry maize stalk as he finds someone to focus on and directs every word to them, just after a searing bolt of lightning tears the house to pieces)

It heralds
the coming lightning wings
when the clouds
gather where far away roads pierce into the sky

They once were alive
They once were the last
We thought would ever fall down away in such a hurry,

(The dancer dances a short story about how man sometimes forgets to see the that sky hovers everlasting, its eye so wide and engulfing, the dancer is asking the sky to reveal what it witnessed. Music)

3

(The poet makes his way through to his place, entranced by the dancer's conversation with the memory of the sky)

generators of spirit

(Silence. The drummer accompanies these words, as the poet tells us about what we see of Massgravedigger doing)

the nudge

of the future ready to rise
because the sparkling words/ falling today
massgravedigger is fingering these coins

called Past,
and she is poking them,

(The dancer, as she pokes into her own pockets)

WOULDN'T you also dare everyone to look into the
                                   bristles of the sun
Wouldn't you preach that we must abandon the hunt
                                        for treasures,
Wouldn't you also loose patience with children that
                        cannot draw a barbed shard or the
Thorns in their windings

When ever-ever-after just became
too bright to see the more we picked up
that the end was coming in such a thronging hurry?

(Come in, Big Thick Voice from between the coins while
Massgravedigger fingers more profusely as if they would give up
gallons of golden blood)

Big Thick Voice:

        lets open this doorframe
into your home

        behold
a mosaic of emotionless faces
stiffer than your tale
about the suffocation of dreams.

lets open this noise that says nothing in the end
like
the door is a contraceptive,

reeking of wreath or confession of pus
inside a pimple mole, swelling
rising, rising.

Since you took the time to ask
I am the one that creeps
behind your shadow

*(As if each knows the precise arrangement of the wires of the
other's thinking sparks, they all become an electric choir to say)*

*shesha, shesha, naba oGqoka 'sambe
bejikeleza okwamandoni, okwezinkonjane*

we've seen
dancers in the air thronging
with screeches of an evil song

*(The dancer extricates himself, as if pissed off that they are talk-
ing about dancer, someone like her)*

we've turned
our hidden video recorder on, but it
only recants its red eye baton

I am saying here, yourunning
andyourunningandyourunningaway,

saying the memories are

trudging through my temples

saying I am upstart for the answers
to the cymbals of your questions,

shadows behind your shadow, winking.

plug your ears always
but this is the original flame an anchor,

*(Ndramas plods across, cancelling the central bond between the
members of our chorus. We can see this because each one
struggles to find a new reason to be alive)*

there are
many worlds, each of which
must breathe and claim
 a space, depending where plant your ears and stand
there so many echoes

my bluepurple greengold flames
grown up from the day it was the original
like the first sprout of my bones
sunrise up
from that hard-to-find place

where deeper and undrying wells are
called knowledge/s,

liberate them,

liberate me so that i may find the cure for a crinkling

                                        road

(The poet takes charge of the whole platform, raising the dial of excitement, that inspires the dancer who is being followed by excited lights)

and so it is gossiped also
the seed never hibernates beneath

but crops
and produces

like we shall witness as we get
deeper into the coeliac swamps

the evergreen lush life there eager
to reach us and touch us
gleams,
grass and games
laughs that cut and blend softly
with the air of friendships,

if it was a see-saw
as when seen you saw
when I fell off

I will know,
ginqi-gonqo

ginqi-gonqo

these things come piss and pass,

so if also

deep in the swamps of your stomach
grows weeds
and travel to your head
and if it all
seeks asylum between my teeth?

liberate it.
liberate it. We are
liberating ourselves in the walking distance
to the post office.

5

(Bende contorts himself into a figure that resembles a self-made wire television set. All watch him as if they were watching a repeat performance of the main clown, the crowd puller of a travelling circus show. Bende has deep feeling that the time has for him to tell us all we need to know about the world that has died. Remember, he is talking about something he has no slight idea of)

It was many years after hackers burners killers' rampage when you saw the hobo careless legs, massgravedigger come limping /full of flames of memory. The memories walk with her words, these tributary habits of words that we saw fold and roll back from her tongue and roll again behind her tongue like three.

(Massgravedigger utters for first time, a croak that makes us wish we will never grow old)

Boot size history, where I love a cracked road. Here used to live the cobbler, there and there him and her, the washer room humming, water splashing, street sweeper lolling there, the governor

dreaming of the town's whorer, who slept as if heaven was her pil-
low He woke up and said cut down all the fig trees

The death could then see everyone clearly
Did they all die when they wanted to, this question is
Too heavy?

6

*(The dancer highlights the main actions. A haunting cello leads the
music. It has become the string pulling together the different
speeches of all that is happening on stage. The dancer interprets
this music as she speaks, softly as if into the ear of a love the she
loves like no other. The cello massages her fantasy. The cello
cares about the dancer)*

Feeling deeper
into the abyss of her aged wounds massgravedigger
discovered that nothing follows
after emptiness, when
the wells of mothers are dry

Big girl don't cry
Big boy don't cry

boy and girl had seen a skull being trampled on
now boy and girl don't breathe
or wish anymore that when
the ice cream comes it comes dripping red

*(Sound of ice-cream kombie's search for buyers. It lasts for a sig-
nificant time to irritate us and distract the insides of our hearts.
Those of us who once heard this sound and wished that like the*

children next door, someone around would give a bulky fifty cents
coin and send us off into a world of cold sweet ice-cream skating)

… people go by
people go by
and then stop just going by stop feigning a supernatural

patience

at last it has come to and we all agree upon it
it's the boiling point in the *proemdramatic,*

we are going to show you
mosquito jag
jou vabbond!

(Violence is unleashed as madness upon the stage, one side is
retreating, the other is forever advancing. It is confusing because
within this great violence, there is an extended unsuccessful
dance, attempting to kill a mosquito, everyone is mumbling curs-
es in afrikaans and other languages. They turn to each other and
they enjoy killing each other as if this was the heightened moment
in a mass orgy taking place at Ellis Park Stadium)

7

(Ndramas and Bende speak this together, as the music gets softer,
and the end of the world brings a quiteness that just says, nothing
exists, so that is how that world ended. Everyone else paces about
like undeparted souls asking for the route to somewhere, any-
where. This is so sad because there is no one to point to where you

the final resting place is located, like hanging horse meat biltong,
this is the end that was completed)

A scrawny placard
from millions of us
who scratch on scabs of ice or
chew on the haunting rings
of cockroach stomachs,

less sonorous than the upwelling
thrusts of hearts gurgling blood,

and when we smile corrosive smiles
smile and count how slowly the years have gone,

slowing years somewhere
in this night trembling, we are together,
to have swallowed

a dry bone,

somewhere beyond this view our heads ring i am not a
                                        stone i am not a stone
see gushing floods of my expectations, take a picture of
                                        me sleeping

in the arcade of automatic bank machines,

(The poet speaks from the back, while the rest act out the story
of the unemployment queue. It is the only thing one can do to
keep sane, it seems they will be here in this vacuum of a place,
just after the end, the resting does not seem to exist)

Welcome to the kingdom ruled by
What is there after the last number, it is cold here
Frontline mouths agog
Your mouths drying up,

cuts in the stomach,
the phone that rings hunger in the stomach.

*(The story of the unemployment queue continues and peaking with
the existential crisis, everyone is itching, uselessness is an itchy
feeling. Music. It ends with everyone exiting from the stage. The
fresh, open grave dominates our vision. It is lit with the orange of
a rising and setting sun)*

<u>contorted silences</u>

*(The poet comes in, his attire is different from what we have seen
him in so far, his narrative is supported by images from a slide
show and complete silence)*

As the sun skids
behind the clouds
shapes and shadows faint

sometimes i know that shadows will lengthen with the day,
though these days one can never be certain

the shade i knew did not stoop like this

like a red dripping cloud
imprinting shapes of terror

or whoosh away
to make way for a still born dawn

or just threaten us all
with thirst and sickness and no sugar
for the tea when the neighbour comes in
to visit me

*(The dancer emerges and leads the story about a people who
were so unlucky that all the time they were left with nothing but
pieces in their hands. The story includes section where a man
goes to buy a packet of Rainbow Farms chicken pieces from the
spaza shop)*

With pieces in our hands

walking, walking walking –

there never was rivers
forming out of tap-dance teardrops

runlets
follow
one another
from necropolis to necropolis

of us who remain ready like a new stove
of this bloom of petals and blood / pieces

razor dreams, like a rat

shuffling in and out

my head's inside,

do like a rat
nibble
and blow cool breeze over the sore

long dry tale, tentacles and ambling things,
suck strength
lock breath

staple my scrotum to the thighs, how i walk
i carry my heads on my head and stalk,

through the clouds hugging and fondling each other

while we wade another the dry water, together we sang

                                           hard

and created new stories about the
going of a driest season, did not help

      a bloom of petals and blood,
fluttering fluorescent under a satellite
rainshower,

      tick tick
and tick tock

      behind the masks
behind the concrete shrouds, behind cotton wool words,

it is a comedy without characters,
the buffoonery is done and curtains are going rend,

and there will be fingers that will poke

at speeches of dead meat. everything is finished.

refugeed

(Bende paces vibrantly, all over the stage. He is moving with the aggression of a headless chicken, fresh with confusion after the neck was wrung. He moves with the determination that today is the day he will find his lost head)

I come to you bruised and scabbed
but I come to you unshackled

I come to you clothed in dots and bloodclots
but I come your way anyway

forever and beyond, we
waited

now

we come to you when our tomb's unveiled
by a lifeless cortège

the day when earth and us would embrace warmly never

came

so

we come to you
knowing how our minds in cast and crutches
hobble about
their regular duties.

(Silence and solemn music of the cello going solo on an empty stage, there are visuals of the cost of forgiving on the screen. Cut to archive footage of the Soyuz spaceship launching off some place in Russia)

bengithi / bathi exit

(The poet is seated as if relating a fireside tale. He is dressed like a space cadet. The cast comes in slowly one-by-one and take up frozen positions in different parts of the stage. Their gaze is set on massgravedigger, who is acting out her part. It looks like we are in space)

So the sun went orange, back to the loving arms of its
mothers and kin. massgravedigger saw herself blow up . saw
pieces of exploded flesh, saw the dust of her bones, she saw a
scorched cortex worm, at the speed of pus, its way into ulcerat-
ed soil. massgravedigger surveyed the aftermath and said

not yet. she said, not yet, whose is this very beautiful head?

(The rest of the cast ignores her and vacates the stage. Massgravedigger implores them to stay. The poet continues)

fragments/ petals/ perilous/
bright heads of children, massgravedigger made a world

      of bright heads, bright like children and

            funny, these were her own dreams

there she goes
burdened

limping
limping

fractured and
moving
to the loneliest
whisper
of the loneliest winds

(It is hard to make out, but it seems like what the rest of cast is humming as they leave, is the hymn – Koloi ya Elia, hayi duma ya tsamaya, e kena ditabeng tsa Zion...)

of us who remain/ petals/ fragments/ of this bloom of petals of
blood of all
the things
that we just must let go

(The Koloi ya Elia hymn continues. Curtains fall. We fade to a blackout. The proemdrama has come to the end.)

My lover still blows

music
of my ear
a water
stare,
spent
rooms
can be hostile
to unaccompanied words,

air stones

bread with a beard

just lying there

wrinkles in my ear
drum's skin
that hum next door
absent love blowing through,

whose furious fingers fasten
as they

fold out.